ARE YOU BORED WITH YOUR COOKING?
ARE YOU LACKING IN PEP?
ARE YOU WATCHING YOUR WEIGHT?

The Yogurt Cookbook offers tasty and healthful solutions to these problems.

Over 100 recipes feature this natural "wonder" food, spanning your menu from appetizer to dessert. Whether you feel like whipping up simple pancakes or an exotic beef Stroganoff or a yogurt pie, you'll find a dish to suit every occasion in this unique collection of delectable and nutritious taste treats.

The
Yogurt
Cookbook

Olga Smetinoff

decorations by Erwin Schachner

PYRAMID BOOKS • **NEW YORK**

THE YOGURT COOKBOOK

A PYRAMID BOOK
Published by arrangement with Frederick Fell, Inc.

Fourth printing April, 1976

Library of Congress Catalog Card Number: 65-23871

ISBN: 0-515-02417-1

Printed in the United States of America

Pyramid Books are published by Pyramid Publications (Harcourt Brace Jovanovich). Its trademarks, consisting of the word "Pyramid" and the portrayal of a pyramid, are registered in the United States Patent Office.

PYRAMID PUBLICATIONS
(Harcourt Brace Jovanovich)
757 Third Avenue
New York, New York 10017, U.S.A.

Dedicated to My Husband
for his prodding, patience and cooperation

CONTENTS

Yogurt

Salads & Dressings

Soups......

Pancakes, Omelets, Casserdes....

Meat, Poultry, Fish....

Vegetables......

International Dishes..

Fruits & Desserts

Cakes Muffins Pies Biscuits

The Yogurt Cookbook

YOGURT

Yogurt in various forms has been used by human beings for over four thousand years. There is evidence in Genesis that both Abraham and Moses served it to their guests, and it was one of the many foods eaten by the ancient Hebrews. The Egyptians knew yogurt; the epicures of old India also knew and used it. Genghis Khan fed it to his armies and even used it as a meat preservative. Emperor Francis I, of France, called it "the milk of life eternal."

Today, many famous and well-known people drink and eat yogurt. In Europe, and particularly Eastern Europe, yogurt is as well-known and used as ham and eggs or coffee and doughnuts in America.

Yogurt, for all of its antiquity and widespread use, is a relatively new phenomenon in the United States.

What sets yogurt apart from such products as clabber or fermented milk is its bacteria—or special organisms. Yogurt has about 200,000,000 bacteria to the cubit centimeter; the organism is known as *Lactobacillus bulgaricus*.

Yogurt is arrived at through the introduction of this culture (or bacterium) into ordinary milk at a controlled temperature; the bacteria are allowed to multiply freely until the milk has the proper consistency, then it is refrigerated.

These healthful bugs work on the harmful bacteria that are present in a person's intestinal tract. They change the flora of the intestines and help clean you out. Yogurt also provides the digestive tract with an extra quantity of lactic acid which is beneficial for good health. Yogurt can be of great help to a sensitive stomach, because over 90 percent is digestible within one hour, compared to 30 percent in milk. It also helps keep the stomach free of harmful bacteria that are present by reason of undigested food.

Served cold, yogurt has the consistency of custard, but if stirred with a spoon, it turns to liquid. It has a tart flavor, snowy-white color, and a faint sourish aroma.

Europeans like their yogurt sweetened with honey or fruit as a dessert. It has been used as a drink, a dressing for salads and vegetables, a sauce for meat, as well as a dessert. In short, yogurt has been a staple article of food in Europe for hundreds of years.

There are claims that yogurt has aided thousands of people suffering from ulcers, allergies, arthritis, and other ailments. It is known that among Bulgarians, who eat a great deal of yogurt, a large percentage of people live to be a hundred years old.

Yogurt is very often called "one of the five wonder foods of the world."

Yogurt is good for people of all ages—children love it—but it is especially beneficial for older people.

For those dieting it is essential not only to lose excess weight, but to maintain health and vitality. Often, people trying to reduce will say, "Oh, I can't drink milk or eat dairy foods, they're fattening." Yet a large glass of yogurt has a very low caloric content. *Yogurt is not fattening.*

The history of yogurt goes back thousands of years. Because my parents came to America from the eastern part of the old country, yogurt in various forms has been a part of my life. When it became popular in America, I became interested in and curious about its origin. I have been studying the fascinating history of yogurt for many years. In writing this book, it was my feeling that many readers would also be interested in this subject. Here is what I found:

Yogurt is a cultured milk. It has a piquant flavor. It was first used in this country as a health food, and is now undergoing a renaissance in a delightful new form—as a glamour ingredient in gourmet cooking. Eastern chefs have been using yogurt as an ingredient for ages. It improves the flavor of food it is made a part of. Yogurt enhances cereals—rice, wheat, corn dishes—blends well in dressings for salads, vegetables, fruits, and makes tangier sauces. Yogurt is an excellent supplement to a diet.

I learned, among other facts, that yogurt has been used for upward of four thousand years. Different countries have different names for it, but it is the same food. The Russians refer to it as *prostokvasha,* and the Bulgarians call it *kiselo mleko.* It is a staple food all the way from Odessa to Peking. It is known in all the Arabic countries of Europe and North Africa. The eminent scientist and Nobel Prize winner, Dr. Ilya Metchnikoff, was a Russian bacteriologist. A member of the Pasteur Institute in Paris, he is the author of *The Prolongation of Life; Old Age;* and *The Nature of Man.* He was the person who first identified the bacilli that created yogurt, thus making it possible to process the food on a mass scale.

Dr. Metchnikoff wrote that the most important fact is that the bacteria found in yogurt manufacture generous amounts of the B vitamins in the digestive tract where they are absorbed and distributed throughout the body.

Yogurt contains certain bacteria that, in the intestinal tract, break down milk sugar into lactic acid in which disease-producing bacteria are unable to live.

Dr. Metchnikoff attributes the longevity and stamina of the people of the Balkan countries to this marvelous food. He found that although they were among the poorest peoples in the world, and were deprived of most of the foods normally containing the necessary vitamins, they were practically immune to stomach troubles. Ulcers were almost unknown. He gave credit for their good health and long lives to yogurt. He found, during the time he conducted this important study, that there were 1,600 Bulgarians over the age of a hundred to every million of population, compared to only 11 Americans per million.

Eleanor Roosevelt stated in a magazine article that she once told her doctor that she eats and likes yogurt. Her doctor's reply was, "Fine. Keep it up. Yogurt is good—and good for you."

Jimmy Durante, the popular comedian, said that he eats a pint of yogurt every day; that it keeps him active, healthy, and full of vitality.

Other famous yogurt fans are: The Duke and Duchess of Windsor, Gloria Swanson, Anthony Eden.

My parents came from the old country. One of my very early recollections and observations is that of an object wrapped up in a blanket on top of the oven. An unveiling revealed an earthen bowl containing yogurt. My mother always had a batch of yogurt developing in a bowl on top of the oven in our kitchen.

We were a large, old-fashioned family and the mainstay of our diet was yogurt. We had our bad times and our good times, but no matter how scanty or bountiful were our provisions, Mother always had a bowl of yogurt growing and developing which was later cooled in the icebox and converted into exciting, exotic dishes or consumed in other ways. Many of the recipes contained in this book were used by my mother and grandmother.

The folks in the old country had no such things as incubators, thermometers, and other expensive gadgets to aid them in making yogurt. The know-how was handed down from one generation to the next. Virtually every household had a "starter" reserved in a cool place for the next batch.

However, the foregoing notwithstanding, since we are living in an electronic age, there is a modern method of preparing yogurt in an electric yogurt maker which I have tried out and found to be practical and efficient. It is a handy tool to have in the kitchen. In the following chapter, I will tell you how to make yogurt at home the way I do it.

How to make yogurt at home

It is universally agreed that yogurt has wonderful merits, but it is costly to buy. Why not make it yourself—at home? It's simple—for one-fourth the cost! You don't need expensive incubators. You don't need expensive thermometers. Here is the original Bulgarian method which will cut the cost of yogurt 75 percent.

To make 1 quart of yogurt:

1 quart milk

3 heaping tablespoons yogurt (commercial variety)

Heat milk until it almost reaches the boiling point. Pour into earthen bowl. Cool until it is warmer than lukewarm, or until milk feels hot when you put a few drops on your wrist. It should feel hot but not burn. (If milk is too hot the organism grows faster, but the curd may be too thick and tough.) Add yogurt (room temperature), stirring gently. Cover bowl and place on warm blanket. Wrap blanket completely around bowl and let stand for at least five hours. (If it is more practical, let yogurt stand overnight.) Place in refrigerator. *Always* reserve ½ cup yogurt to be used as a culture (or yeast) for the next batch. You need buy yogurt only once; however, if your yogurt becomes too thin, start again with fresh commercial yogurt.

And that isn't all—make your own real, smooth pot cheese. Make a bag of unbleached muslin or doubled cheesecloth, hem the top and draw a string through it. Place 1 quart (or less) of yogurt in the bag. Hang the bag by tying it on to the faucet over the sink overnight. In the morning remove the cheese from the bag. It is snowy white and delicious; it lends itself to many variations:

Add freshly ground pepper and blend well; flavor with herbs—basil, dill, parsley, garlic, and paprika. Caraway seeds add piquancy and a flavor that is really unusual.

Use homemade pot cheese as a filling for sandwiches; for salads over lettuce and vegetables.

Wash and remove stem part of green bell pepper, hollow out. Mix enough pot cheese with finely chopped walnuts and stuff pepper. Place in covered dish in refrigerator and chill thoroughly (overnight, if possible). Slice with sharp knife and use as a filling for sandwiches.

Friends who have traveled extensively in European countries report with enthusiasm and pleasure that of all the beverages served in restaurants, coffee shops, snack bars, etc., yogurt is the most popular. In large cities as well as in smaller communities, yogurt combined with fruit in an electric blender is consumed more than any other food either as a beverage or a separate course.

In the Middle East a dish of yogurt, often spiced with herbs, is served as a prelude to a full-course meal as an aid to digestion.

Tired of conventional breakfasts? Try scrambled eggs with yogurt:

Sauté two peeled, chopped tomatoes in butter until cooked, add salt and pepper. Beat 4 eggs slightly, pour into tomatoes and stir constantly until the eggs are cooked. Spoon yogurt over eggs and either heat through or place about 4 inches from broiler flame for a few minutes to heat.

Note: Yogurt should be at room temperature for cooking purposes.

Many years after I had left "the nest," so to speak, and was on my own, I patronized a couple who owned a cleaning store. The man and his wife were in their middle years, short of stature, had been in the United States only a few years and had scarcely learned to speak English.

They attended to customers in the front part of the store and cut, sewed and pressed in the rear under artificial light surrounded by bundles and clothes hangers bulging with clothing. They toiled from very early in the morning until late at night —often until midnight.

The language barrier notwithstanding, their business flourished, for they were indeed skilled at their trade.

I recall experiencing a renewed shock every time I visited their establishment. It was difficult for me to reconcile their wholesome appearance, their sunny dispositions, and their overwhelming vitality with the grueling work in which they were engaged. Both had black, glossy hair, sparkling dark eyes, and the very whitest, well-shaped teeth imaginable.

Since personal sewing and cleaning needs brought me to their store frequently, I became quite friendly with them. One day I asked them how they were able to work so hard and such long hours every day (including Sundays if they had special orders to finish) and maintain their health; how they were always so cheerful and spry; how, since they were always indoors, their complexions were so good; why their hair and eyes shone; in short, why they looked as if they had been playing tennis in the sunshine instead of stitching away long, long hours.

They laughed and invited me to follow them into their back room. They led me to a small kitchen table, where they usually had their meals, and removed a blanket from a board which covered a number of glasses of what appeared to be milk. They informed me that the secret of their good health and fine appearance was in the contents of those glasses; that they each consumed six glasses daily. They offered me some of it and I recognized immediately that it was the same yogurt that had been the mainstay of our diet in the home of my parents. They explained that it would be impossible for them to carry on were it not for this wonder food. They had been using it ever since they could remember in their native Armenia, along with the rest of their people, and when they arrived in America they brought their habits and know-how with them. Although there were periods in their lives when they could afford little else, they knew that as long as they drank and ate yogurt they would remain in good health and be able to make a living.

The wife told me that every evening before they left their business she made a fresh batch of yogurt, pouring the heated milk into a dozen glasses, along with a little yogurt from the previous batch as a starter, and covered the glasses with a board over which she placed a warm blanket. In the morning they had delicious health-giving food either to eat in various forms or to drink.

My mother had done the same thing years ago, using a large earthen bowl instead. Now, I do the same for my own family.

How to use yogurt

Many restaurants that specialize in foods of the Near East serve yogurt as a first course—as an aid to digestion.

Try drinking a glass of yogurt when you are extremely tired—discover how it will perk you up.

To vary the taste of yogurt, add a spoonful or two of fruit juice; crushed fruit or berries (strawberries, raspberries, etc.), maple syrup, or honey.

Place 1 tablespoon frozen grape concentrate on top of a serving of chilled yogurt. For variety use any of the juice concentrates. For a colorful and delicious dessert fill an attractive glass dish with yogurt and place a tablespoon of frozen orange, apricot, papaya, pineapple juice, Hawaiian punch, or guava (any of these delightful concentrates) on top. The taste contrast is unique and exciting.

Pour yogurt mixed with herbs over cottage cheese, sliced bananas or other fruit, berries, or melon balls.

Boil small potatoes in their jackets, peel and cover with yogurt to which parsley, chives, or watercress has been added. Or try mincing a small clove of garlic to add to the yogurt.

Spoon yogurt over stewed prunes or apricots or any dried fruit.

For unusual desserts (slimming, too—yogurt contains only 155 calories per cup compared to 445 calories in other dairy products) mix 1 cup of yogurt with 2 tablespoons of powdered sugar and a few drops of vanilla or fresh lemon juice. Whip until frothy. This is an excellent topping for fruit desserts.

Slice hard-boiled eggs; cover with yogurt which has been mixed with a little mayonnaise and chili sauce. Sprinkle with parsley.

Combine 1 cup cooked diced carrots, 1 cup cooked peas. Mix with ¾ cup of yogurt. Serve cold on a bed of lettuce.

The flavor of yogurt is enhanced by adding minced garlic, paprika, etc. Use with a light hand.

Use spices and herbs to create exotic flavors and piquancy; saffron over rice for color and taste; basil, dill, parsley, and paprika.

Tuna fish or salmon (canned) is a good luncheon dish. Combined with yogurt it can be served cold or mixed and baked in a 300-degree oven until heated through.

Avocado and cottage cheese, topped with yogurt which has been seasoned with garlic salt and paprika, is a healthful combination.

With yogurt there is really no end of flavor possibilities. Yogurt slightly sweetened with honey or fruit juice, served with berries or fruit and whipped up in an electric blender is but a beginning.

One can go on from this simple start plus a little imagination to create the most amazing foods.

Yogurt lends itself to limitless variations—combine with chopped olives, watercress, chives, dill, and parsley.

Mix yogurt with tomato juice and add a few drops of lemon juice to taste.

Combine yogurt with apples, oranges and celery.

Baked apples with a yogurt topping are piquant.

Pickled herring that may be purchased commercially served with yogurt is a good luncheon dish.

Experiment with yogurt. It lends itself to many variations.

Use yogurt instead of sour cream or buttermilk; yes, even in place of regular milk to give your pancakes, waffles, cookies, and cakes a tangier taste.

Use an electric blender

The following combinations may be mixed with a manual egg beater in a bowl, or shaken up in a covered jar, but for the best results use an electric blender for smooth consistency. It is superior in every way and will save time:

Mix together 2 cups yogurt, 1 cup orange juice and 1 tablespoon sugar.

Cook potatoes in salted water until tender. Mix with a raw, peeled, cut cucumber; sprinkle with parsley and add yogurt. Mix well. This may be served either as a hot or a cold soup.

Mix together 1 cup yogurt, 2 cups uncreamed cottage cheese, 2 teaspoons sugar, 1/3 cup orange juice and 1 teaspoon vanilla. Blend until fluffy. Serve over bananas, berries, orange slices, peaches and sliced melon.

Blend yogurt and grated beets—or cut beets into small pieces, add yogurt and blend until frothy (use either raw or cooked beets).

Here is a healthful, delicious drink recipe for children:

2 cups yogurt
1 egg yolk
2 tablespoons sugar
1 tablespoon lemon juice
1 tablespoon jelly (strawberry, raspberry, cherry)

Note: Yogurt mixed with canned, frozen fruits, berries, and vegetables in an electric blender is an easy and speedy way to prepare food.

SALADS & DRESSINGS

Yogurt dressings

½ cup yogurt
1 avocado
½ clove garlic, mashed fine
1 teaspoon lemon juice, or to taste

Mash avocado in small bowl, add other ingredients, and beat until thick consistency. Serve over crisp lettuce.

1 cup yogurt
   Juice of 1 lemon
   Sugar, to taste

½ cup yogurt
½ cup mayonnaise
   Juice of ½ lemon or a little vinegar
   Sugar, to taste

½ cup yogurt
½ cup mayonnaise
   Lemon juice, to taste (or vinegar)
   Sugar, to taste
1 tablespoon ketchup or chili sauce

Yogurt dressings for reducers

½ cup yogurt
½ cup tomato juice (or less depending
   on thickness desired)
Lemon juice, a few drops

Combine yogurt, a little honey, a pinch of salt and a little lemon juice. Beat all ingredients together. Serve with any raw or cooked vegetable salad. Vary by including chopped green olives, watercress, chives, dill, parsley.

Minced garlic—let your taste determine the amount—will add a pleasant flavor to your dressings.

Cole slaw

1 cup yogurt
¼ cup vinegar
½ cup mayonnaise
3 cups cabbage, shredded
2 medium beets, canned or cooked
Sugar, salt and pepper to taste

Place cabbage in large bowl, add vinegar, and sprinkle with sugar. Let stand for a while. Add chopped beets, salt and pepper. Mix yogurt with mayonnaise and blend in with other ingredients. Chill thoroughly before serving.

1 cup yogurt
¼ cup mayonnaise
2 tablespoons vinegar or lemon juice
3 cups cabbage
1 carrot, grated
Sugar to taste
⅛ teaspoon salt

Wash cabbage; place in refrigerator until crisp; shred; grate carrot. Combine yogurt, mayonnaise, sugar, salt, and vinegar or lemon juice. Mix thoroughly with cabbage and carrot.

Cole Slaw (No. 2)

      1 cup yogurt (about)
    ¼ cup mayonnaise
    ¼ cup vinegar
      3 cups washed, crisp, shredded cabbage
  1½ cups beets, diced (cooked or canned)
    ½ bell pepper, cut fine
      Sugar, salt and pepper to taste

Mix cabbage, beets, and bell pepper together; add sugar, salt and pepper to taste. Blend well yogurt, mayonnaise, and vinegar; pour over cabbage mixture. Serve immediately if you like the cabbage crisp, or allow to stand in refrigerator for a while to soften.

Anchovy salad

    1 cup yogurt
    2 small cans anchovy flat fillets
    1 green pepper
  ½ cup celery, cut fine
    1 green onion, cut fine
      Chopped parsley or dill
      Vinegar

Combine anchovy fillets (reserving oil in cans) with green pepper, tomatoes, celery and onion. Mix vinegar with oil in anchovy cans (enough to fill cans). Pour over combined salad. Serve over crisp lettuce leaves. Sprinkle with parsley or dill and top with yogurt.

Crabmeat salad

   1 cup yogurt
   ¼ cup chili sauce
   1 tablespoon lemon juice
     Canned or cooked crabmeat

Mix yogurt, chili sauce and lemon juice well. Add crabmeat (shredded if canned) broken up into small pieces. Either fold in yogurt dressing or serve crabmeat on crisp lettuce leaves and serve dressing separately.

European (Turkish) salad

   4 or 5 cucumbers (sliced)
   2 cups yogurt
      Water
      Salt and pepper

Add enough water to blend with yogurt for desired consistency. Slice cucumbers very thin, add seasoning. Pour blended yogurt over cucumbers and chill for several hours.

Molded beet salad

    Yogurt
1 package lemon Jello
1 cup boiled water
    Juice from 1 can beets and enough
    boiling water to make ¾ cup
¾ cup celery (cut fine)
1 can diced beets (16 ounces)
1 tablespoon vinegar

Dissolve Jello in boiling water, add beet juice and vinegar. When Jello thickens slightly, add beets. Place in refrigerator for several hours. Top with yogurt.

Danish cucumber salad

Yogurt
2 medium cucumbers
2 tablespoons very hot water
¾ cup vinegar
3 tablespoons sugar
Salt and pepper to taste
1 teaspoon fresh or dried basil or oregano

Cut cucumber in very thin slices (peel if desired). Heat water, sugar and vinegar together, add salt and pepper. Add cucumbers, sprinkle with basil or oregano and let cool for about 10 minutes. Place in refrigerator to chill. Top with yogurt.

Potato salad

Yogurt, ¾ cup
8 small potatoes
½ cup mayonnaise
1 tablespoon oil
3 tablespoons vinegar
2 hard-boiled eggs, cut up
1 small onion, chopped fine
3 tablespoons celery, cut fine
Parsley, chopped fine
Salt and pepper to taste

Boil potatoes in skins in salted water; cool, peel, and dice. Cover with oil and vinegar. Let stand until marinated. Add celery, eggs and onion, salt and pepper to taste. Beat yogurt with mayonnaise and add to potato mixture. Mix well. Sprinkle with parsley. Refrigerate for some time before serving.

There are many methods of making potato salad, but the above recipe is something special.

A more simple one is to mix the potatoes, onion, celery, chopped parsley, and seasonings. Mix with yogurt dressing (as above). Omit the eggs. Serve.

Avocado mixes & dips

    ½ cup yogurt
     1 large avocado
     3 tablespoons lemon juice
       Garlic powder and salt to taste

Mash avocado, add lemon juice and seasonings; add yogurt and beat up well.

Combine and mix well 1 package of dehydrated onion soup with 1 cup of yogurt. Add more yogurt if a thinner consistency is desired.

Piquant mix

   1 cup yogurt
   1 tablespoon ketchup or chili sauce
   1 small clove garlic
   1 tablespoon horseradish
     Hard-boiled egg, grated
   1 tablespoon chopped parsley
     Scallions, chopped fine

Mash garlic very fine and mix with yogurt, ketchup or chili sauce, horse-radish, egg, and parsley. Sprinkle with scallions and paprika to add piquancy and color.

This may be served as an appetizer or a dip.

Yogurt blended with minced garlic makes a good mix—add a little water for a thinner consistency and it becomes a healthful drink.

Egg & lettuce salad

½ cup yogurt
½ cup mayonnaise
2 tablespoons lemon juice
Minced garlic
1 teaspoon salt
Paprika
2 hard-boiled eggs
1 crisp head of lettuce

Mix the dressing (yogurt, mayonnaise, lemon juice, salt) together. Separate crisp leaves of lettuce and dry thoroughly. Pour dressing over leaves, slice eggs and sprinkle generously with paprika and serve; or arrange sliced eggs over lettuce leaves and spoon dressing over salad; sprinkle with paprika.

Combination salad

2 cups yogurt
2 cucumbers, peeled and cubed
2 tomatoes, cut up
Small bunch of scallions (green onions)
cut fine
Small bunch of red radishes, sliced
Carton of cottage cheese
Salt to taste
Paprika

Combine cucumbers, scallions, tomatoes, radishes in a large salad bowl and salt to taste. Mix well. Divide into the number of individual portions desired and serve on lettuce leaves with a generous helping of cottage cheese. Spoon yogurt over salad and sprinkle with paprika for color and health.

Fish & vegetable salad

  ½ cup yogurt
  ¼ cup vinegar
  2 tablespoons ketchup
  Lemon juice to taste
  1 small can fish (tuna or salmon)
  ½ cup diced celery
  ½ cup diced cucumbers
  Salt and pepper to taste

Beat yogurt, vinegar, ketchup, and lemon juice together. Flake fish (or break up into bite-size pieces), add celery and cucumbers. Fold in dressing.

Party salad

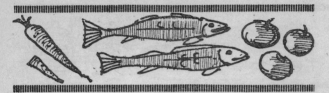

    1 cup yogurt
    2 herrings (about 1 pound each)
2½ cups cooked, cold diced potatoes
    2 cups cooked, (or canned) cold diced beets
    2 tablespoons finely chopped onion
    3 tart apples, diced
1½ cups diced cooked carrots
      Salad greens, cut up

Dressing: Yogurt, ⅓ cup vinegar, 2 tablespoons sugar, ½ teaspoon pepper.

Garnish: 2 hard-cooked eggs, chopped, ⅓ cup chopped beets.

Clean and soak fish overnight in cold water. Remove skin and bones carefully. Cut fillets into thin strips 1 to 2 inches long. Combine herring, potatoes, beets, carrots, onion, apples. Mix together ingredients for dressing, add to salad and toss lightly. Chill for several hours. Garnish before serving with chopped eggs and beets. The above salad takes a little doing, but it is worth it.

Chopped herring

Yogurt
2 salt herrings
1 small onion
3 hard-boiled eggs
¼ cup white vinegar
1 white roll (soft part)
Sugar

Soak herring in water to cover overnight. Change water twice. Drain and fillet. Either chop the fillets, onion, and two eggs, or put through grinder. Add roll which has been soaking in vinegar, a little sugar, and chop until finely mixed. Top with yogurt.

This may be used as an appetizer, spread, or a dip.

Cauliflower salad

1 cup yogurt
¼ cup mayonnaise
1 cauliflower
Parsley, salt and pepper

Soak cauliflower in a little salted water for a few minutes. Wash well and boil in salted water until tender (5 to 8 minutes). Break up into flowerets. Chill well and serve with yogurt blended with mayonnaise. Sprinkle with parsley.

Zucchini salad

    1 cup yogurt
    1 pound zucchini
       Lemon juice
       Parsley, dill or scallion cut fine
       Sugar

Scrub zucchini under running water (do not peel) and slice very thin. Add chopped parsley, dill, or scallion. Fold in yogurt mixed with lemon juice and a little sugar to taste. Let stand in refrigerator for a time before serving.

Yogurt dressing salad
for a warm day

  1 head of lettuce
  2 hard-boiled eggs
  ½ teaspoon sugar
     Lemon juice or vinegar to taste
     Salt and paprika
     Yogurt

With a sharp knife remove part of core from lettuce; wash well in cold water; drain; refrigerate until chilled and crisp. Mash yolk of 1 egg, add sugar and lemon juice or vinegar to taste, and enough yogurt for desired consistency. Mix well. Cut lettuce into quarters. Pour yogurt mixture over lettuce; garnish with remaining egg and egg white and sprinkle with salt and paprika.

For fruits

Whip equal amounts of yogurt and mayonnaise, add powdered sugar (granulated sugar thins out consistency) and a little vanilla. Fold into salads or use as topping.

SOUPS

Sweet-and-sour cabbage soup

1 small cabbage
1 medium sized onion
2 quarts water
2 cups canned tomatoes (whole)
1 teaspoon salt
Pepper to taste
Juice of 1 lemon (about)
¼ cup sugar
Yogurt

Shred cabbage, dice onion and add to boiling water. Boil very slowly 30 minutes. Add rest of ingredients. Simmer 1½ hours. Taste from time to time to improve flavor by correcting seasonings. Serve soup hot—top with yogurt. The hot soup-cold yogurt combination will appeal to your taste buds.

Cabbage soup cooked with meat

Place 1 pound of beef in 2 quarts of cold water; bring to a boil. Skim off the top. Prepare soup as above. Top with yogurt.

Note: Skim off top of soup frequently for a clear soup.

Variation: Meat may be served as a separate course with the addition of a plain boiled potato.

Borscht

The recipe for borscht is something that is inherited. If you picked the right parents, you developed a taste for it and learned the know-how for making it. In the past, this soup was popular only among certain segments of the population. Currently, however, borscht is served in the finest restaurants and hotel dining rooms. It is nutritious, refreshing, and has definite eye appeal.

2 bunches of beets (about 8)
1 medium onion, chopped (optional)
8 cups water
   Juice of 1 large lemon
3 tablespoons sugar (about)
2 eggs
1 tablespoon salt
   Yogurt

In a large saucepan boil the water. Wash and peel beets; place in boiling water with onion (if desired) and cook over medium heat for 30 minutes, skimming off top at frequent intervals; add lemon juice and sugar. Taste. This soup requires tasting (ideally, it should have a rich sweet-and-sour flavor). Continue cooking and skimming for about 10 minutes longer. Remove beets; grate about six beets and return to soup; cook and stir for a few minutes longer until well mixed.

Beat eggs and salt together in a large bowl until light. Slowly add the soup, a little at a time (to prevent curdling); continue beating. Top generously with yogurt and serve.

Borscht may be served either hot or cold. A favorite touch is a plain hot boiled potato served in either hot or cold soup.

The remaining beets may be served in a salad topped with yogurt, or combined with other cold vegetables in a combination salad.

Note: The simplest method of preparing this soup is to cool it, combine with yogurt, and place in an electric blender until the texture is thick and creamy. Some of the better restaurants use this method.

Variation: Omit the eggs, cool the borscht and either top with yogurt or blend borscht and yogurt in electric blender.

Serve with scallions, cut fine.

Borscht is often prepared without parboiling the beets (as above). Peel and grate 5 large raw beets, cook until tender in 6 cups of water. Proceed in the same manner as above. Potatoes, cooked in their jackets, peeled and served with borscht constitute a complete dish.

If you have never tasted sweet-and-sour meat, you should; it is different. Use about 2 pounds of beef—chuck, brisket—place beets, 2 onions, meat, 8 cups of water in a soup pot, bring to a boil, then simmer until tender (about 2 hours). After meat has been simmering for about 1 hour, add seasonings—sugar, salt, pepper, and lemon juice; a little garlic improves the flavor. About ½ hour before it is finished, add 1 cup of shredded cabbage. Omit egg. Top with yogurt.

Note: Meat may be eaten as a separate course.

For an attractive, clear soup, skim whenever necessary.

Cucumber soup

2 cups yogurt
4 cucumbers
Salt, sugar
2 tablespoons oil
1 teaspoon vinegar (mix with the oil)

Peel cucumbers and cut in thin slices. Season with salt and sugar. Mix with a fork, add oil and vinegar. Fold in yogurt.

Sorrel soup for warm days

Here is a popular, healthful soup which one can find in any household whose parents emigrated from the eastern part of Europe. It has a unique flavor and may be prepared in a variety of ways and served either as a refreshing drink or as a separate course. Served with vegetables accompanied by bread and butter it is a complete meal.

Sorrel, about 2 pounds
2 quarts water
1½ teaspoons salt
4 tablespoons sugar, or to taste
2 tablespoons lemon juice
2 eggs
1 cup yogurt

Wash sorrel thoroughly (the way you would spinach), remove stems, chop. In a large saucepan bring water to a boil, add sorrel and boil rapidly for a few minutes; lower heat and cook gently for about 10 minutes. Add lemon juice and sugar and cook for a few minutes longer (taste and correct seasoning if necessary).

Beat eggs with salt in a large bowl. Add the soup to the well-beaten eggs very gradually to prevent curdling. When cool place in refrigerator.

To serve: float thin slices of cucumber on top and/or sliced scallions. Top with a generous amount of yogurt.

Note: Beaten eggs may be omitted entirely. In an electric blender place cool soup and yogurt and blend until thick and frothy. Hard-cooked eggs may be blended with the combined soup and yogurt.

Note: Should sorrel be unobtainable in your area, this soup may be prepared with spinach.

Note: For cold days, serve sorrel soup hot with yogurt topping.

Quick beet borscht

No. 303 can diced beets
Can of water
4 tablespoons sugar (about)
3 tablespoons lemon juice (to taste)
1 egg
Salt
Yogurt

Combine beets with water, add sugar and bring quickly to a boil; add lemon juice. Cook for about 15 minutes. Taste and correct seasoning.

In a large bowl, beat egg together with salt well. Gradually add beet soup to egg mixture so that it will not curdle. When cool, refrigerate. Top with yogurt and serve.

If an electric blender is used, omit egg, remove some of the beets (use for salad), and add more yogurt. Blend until thick.

PANCAKES
OMELETTES
CASSEROLES

Dinner casserole

*yes, you can cook with yogurt; heating
in no way lessens its healthful qualities*

Here is a complete protein dinner casserole:

   1¼ cups yogurt
   1 cup cottage cheese (dry)
   ¼ cup butter, melted
   ½ teaspoon salt
   ⅛ teaspoon pepper
   1 egg, beaten
   1 package medium broad noodles

Cook noodles until slightly underdone. Drain,
rinse under cold water. Add other ingredients.
Mix and bake in slow oven (300° F.) about 45
minutes.

Is your family tired of cooked cereal for breakfast? Try this nourishing method of serving cereals for a new taste experience. Use the quick cooking variety—rolled oats, Wheatena, corn meal, whole-grain cereals, etc.:

Quick pancake

- 1 cup quick cooking cereal, uncooked
- 1 tablespoon sugar
- ¼ teaspoon soda
- ¼ teaspoon baking powder
- ¼ teaspoon salt
- 1 cup yogurt
- 2 egg yolks
- 2 egg whites
- 1 tablespoon butter

Beat egg whites until stiff but not dry. In another bowl, beat yolks well, add yogurt, mix; add dry ingredients.

Fold in egg whites. Melt tablespoon butter in large frying pan; pile mixture in pan and bake 20 minutes in a moderately hot oven (350° F.). Serve plain or with honey, jam, applesauce, or syrup.

Smoked salmon omelet

Yogurt
4 eggs
1 tablespoon water
1 medium onion (diced)
5 slices smoked salmon
3 tablespoons butter (or margarine)

Sauté onion slowly in butter until brown; place salmon slices on top of onions and cook until salmon turns color, turning fish carefully. Beat eggs with water, season with pepper and a little salt, and pour over fish; cook slowly. When eggs are set, spoon yogurt over eggs and pass briefly under moderate flames of broiler.

Potato pancakes

Yogurt
3 medium potatoes
1 small onion
1 egg
1 teaspoon salt
¼ teaspoon pepper
About 1 tablespoon flour or cracker
meal

Grate potatoes and remove as much of the liquid as possible. Grate onion. Add other ingredients—batter should not be too thick. Fry immediately in hot fat until crisp and brown. (If oil is used, turn frequently.) Serve with yogurt as a topping.

Yogurt pancakes

1¼ cups flour
1 teaspoon sugar
½ teaspoon salt
Pinch of baking powder
1 teaspoon baking soda
2 egg yolks, beaten
2 egg whites, beaten until stiff but not dry
2 tablespoons melted butter
1 cup yogurt

Sift dry ingredients. Blend together egg yolks and yogurt, mix well; add to dry ingredients, add butter and mix together lightly. Fold in egg whites. Bake on hot greased griddle or heavy pan. Serve with syrup, honey or jelly.

Luncheon pancakes

½ cup yogurt
2 egg yolks
1½ tablespoons flour
¼ pound Swiss cheese (broken into small pieces)
½ teaspoon salt
Butter for frying

Combine all ingredients (except butter), mix well. Melt butter in pan; drop heaping tablespoon of mixture into pan and fry until golden brown on both sides.

Yogurt with stuffed mixed vegetables

1 cup yogurt
1 pound ground meat
3 tablespoons washed rice
¼ cup parsley, chopped
Salt and pepper to taste
Vegetables: zucchini, large tomatoes, green peppers (cabbage leaves, optional)

Scoop out centers of zucchini (if large, cut in half), cut slice from stem end of tomatoes and scoop out pulp, remove seeds from peppers (if cabbage leaves are used, wilt in boiling water). Sprinkle cavities with salt and pepper. Mix together meat, rice and tomato sauce or soup; season well.

Line casserole with vegetables that were scooped out. Arrange stuffed vegetables over scoopings. Cook on top of stove over a very low flame or bake in slow oven for about 1½ hours, depending on the amount. Make sure casserole has a tight cover. No water!

Pass around bowl of yogurt for topping.

Blini

The following takes a little doing, but it's worth the effort:

    2 cups milk
  ½ package yeast
    2 teaspoons sugar
    3 cups sifted flour
    3 eggs, separated
    5 tablespoons butter, melted
  ½ teaspoon salt
    Yogurt

Scald the milk and let cool to lukewarm. Add the yeast and stir until yeast has softened. Add sugar and half the flour; beat well. Cover, set in a warm place until doubled in bulk—about 1½ hours.

Beat egg yolks with the butter and salt. Add to batter. Add remaining flour and beat until smooth. Cover and let rise as previously until doubled in bulk—about ½ hour.

Beat egg whites stiff and fold into batter. Let stand at least ten minutes.

Heat and butter lightly a frying pan or griddle. Use 1 tablespoon of batter for each cake;

bake until golden brown on each side, turning once.

Serve with cottage cheese (small curd, often called farmer style). Top with yogurt which has been beaten with powdered sugar, a few drops of vanilla and a little cinnamon.

Leftover batter (if there is any) may be kept in the refrigerator.

Variations: Blinis may also be served with smoked salmon or with onions and mushrooms sautéed in butter until brown, and topped with generous portions of yogurt.

Truly there are blintzes and blintzes—here is a recipe that is worth the effort:

Blintzes w/yogurt dressing

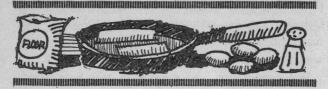

        1   cup flour
    1¼ cups water
        4   eggs
        ½   teaspoon salt

Mix water with flour until paste is smooth (no lumps). Beat eggs well with a fork in a larger bowl. Add eggs to flour mixture and beat well. Pour just enough batter onto slightly greased 6-inch pan (that is not too hot); tilt pan until batter spreads over entire surface. Cook until slightly browned on one side only. Pile onto a kitchen towel until all the cakes are baked.

Blintze Filling

        1   pound pot cheese, dry (often called
            baker's cheese)
        2   eggs
        ½   cup sugar
        ½   teaspoon cinnamon
            Salt to taste

Combine all ingredients. Place 1 heaping table-spoon of filling in center of browned side of each pancake. Fold over all four sides—oblong envelope fashion. Fry on pan or griddle in butter (or margarine) until browned on all sides. Serve hot with yogurt poured over each blintze as eaten.

For expediency and simplicity this is a good method—bake the blintzes. Place the filled blintzes in a well-greased shallow pan and brush each blintze generously with butter (or margarine). Bake in a 350° F. oven for about 30 minutes or until well browned.

Try this variation which is just as delicious but perhaps easier to manage:

Take a loaf of sliced white bread; cut off crusts; roll each slice very thin on a board with a glass or rolling pin and dip it into the following well-mixed batter:

3 eggs
1 cup milk
1 tablespoon sugar
¼ teaspoon salt

Place dipped bread on a plate and put 1 table-spoon of blintze filling in center and fold it up envelope fashion. Fry in butter or shortening—they fry fast—watch them. If these bread blintzes are refrigerated, either overnight or for several hours before frying, they are easy to handle. Top with yogurt. You'll enjoy them.

Baked fish

1 cup yogurt
1 pound fish
1 onion
1 green pepper, sliced
1 tomato, cup up
¼ cup water
 Salt, pepper
3 tablespoons butter (or margarine)

Slice vegetables. Place half of the vegetables on the bottom of a greased baking dish. Season fish with salt and pepper and arrange over bed of vegetables; cover with remaining half. Add water, dot with butter, a little more salt and pepper. Bake for half an hour. Cover with yogurt and heat thoroughly.

Note: Fish steaks, such as halibut, bass, cod, may be broiled in the regular way with lemon and butter; when finished, remove to a hot platter, add yogurt to sauce in pan, stirring constantly. Heat well, but do not boil. Pour sauce over fish.

Kasha, or buckwheat groats, is a grain. It is an excellent source of protein and is an excellent food for energy. It is one of the most popular foods in Russia. Kasha may be obtained in a number of varieties: coarse brown buckwheat groats, whole brown groats, and in the form of kernels. It is a convenience-packaged food, easily and speedily prepared. Use it as a substitute for potatoes and rice, or combine it with cooked noodles. This will prove a welcome addition on your food shelf.

This is a must—try it. It is good—and good for you.

Beef Stroganoff

       2 pounds beef, lean (top round steak)
       1 cup mushrooms (fresh more
         flavorful)
       1 large onion, diced
       5 tablespoons butter
         Flour
         Salt, pepper and paprika
    1½ cups water
         Yogurt

Cut beef across the grain into thin slices about an inch and a half long. Season with salt and pepper. Dip in flour and fry in butter for a short time, turning frequently. Remove to Dutch oven (or any pot with a heavy cover). Fry onions in same butter in pan until almost brown. Add onions and mushrooms (cut into small pieces if large) to meat. Boil the water in same frying pan, stir well, and pour over meat, onions and mushrooms. Cook over low heat until tender. (If meat has been sliced thin, about 40 minutes is enough.) When finished, remove to hot platter or top of double boiler. Mix yogurt with gravy until thoroughly heated on a small flame (stirring constantly) and pour over meat. Serve at once.

Chicken paprika w/yogurt

Chicken 5 pounds or more
1 cup sliced onions
¼ cup shortening, oil, or butter
Flour—about ¼ cup
1 teaspoon salt
3 tablespoons paprika
Hot water to almost cover chicken
Yogurt

Cut cleaned chicken into serving pieces. Shake in bag containing flour, salt and 2 tablespoons paprika. Heat shortening in heavy chicken frying pan or Dutch oven; brown onions, add chicken and brown—turn from time to time. Add water and cook slowly until tender (test degree of tenderness with fork); add the rest of the paprika, cook a little longer. Remove chicken to hot platter. Mix yogurt with gravy until thoroughly heated (stirring constantly), and pour over chicken.

Note: If pressed for time, a roaster or frying chicken will cook much faster.

VEGETABLES

Rice pilaf No. 1

    Yogurt
1 cup rice
3 tablespoons butter
1 small onion, diced
2 cups stock, chicken, beef
    Salt and pepper to taste

Braise rice in 2 tablespoons of melted butter, stirring frequently until butter bubbles and rice is light brown. Fry onion (in remaining butter) in separate pan until brown, add to rice, add stock. Blend well, bake 375° F. for 30 minutes, stir, bake for about 10 minutes longer. Top with yogurt.

Rice pilaf No. 2

        Yogurt
  1 cup rice
  1 small onion
  2 tablespoons butter
  2 cups chicken broth

  Sauté onion until slightly browned; stir in rice and cook slowly, stirring frequently for a few minutes longer. Add chicken broth, cover tightly and cook over low heat until rice absorbs liquid (about 20 minutes). Serve hot covered with yogurt. Sprinkle with saffron or paprika.

Kasha

   1 cup buckwheat groats
   1 egg, beaten
   2 cups water
   1 teaspoon salt
   1 tablespoon shortening (optional)
   Yogurt

Combine egg, groats and salt. In medium-size frying pan (or saucepan) melt shortening; stir in groats mixture, add water; bring to fast boil. Cook, tightly covered, over low heat 15 minutes. Serve topped with yogurt.

Plain kasha

1 cup buckwheat groats
2 cups water
1 teaspoon salt
1 tablespoon butter (optional)
Yogurt

Boil water in a heavy saucepan. Stir in groats, slowly. Add salt and butter. Boil rapidly for 1 minute, cover tightly and simmer for 15 minutes. Top with yogurt.

Fried eggplant

1 eggplant
  Flour
  Egg, beaten with 1 tablespoon water
  Cracker or bread crumbs
  Salt and pepper
  Shortening, oil or butter
  Yogurt

Slice unpeeled eggplant 1/4 inch thick; salt slices for 10 minutes, wipe dry. Dip slices in flour, then beaten egg, and then in crumbs. Fry in butter slowly, or hot oil rapidly until brown. Top with yogurt.

Yogurt and spinach or kale

  ½ cup yogurt
   1 pound spinach or kale
    Salt
    Freshly ground pepper

Steam spinach or kale for a short time until well wilted. Serve cold, topped with yogurt.

Yogurt w/eggplant

  1 cup yogurt
  1 eggplant
  1 tablespoon butter
  1 tablespoon butter (or oil)
   Onions
   Salt
   Pepper

Cube eggplant (salt for about 10 minutes on a board or shallow dish), dry well. Brown onions with seasonings in butter (or oil), add eggplant, and cook uncovered until tender. Add yogurt and heat through.

This dish tastes like sautéed mushrooms.

Yogurt w/zucchini

Scrub and wash zucchini (1 pound) under running water. Cut into very thin slices and sauté in a tightly covered pan in 1 tablespoon of melted butter. Fold in yogurt, heat through and sprinkle with paprika.

Yogurt broiled tomatoes

    ½ cup yogurt
    4 fresh tomatoes
      Bread crumbs
      Garlic salt
      Chopped parsley

Cut tomatoes in half crosswise. Mix yogurt, garlic salt and crumbs and spread over tomatoes. Broil about 4 inches from moderate heat for about 5 minutes, until topping is brown and tomatoes are soft.

Yogurt w/celery and cabbage

1 cup yogurt
3 stalks of celery cut fine, diagonally
1 small head of cabbage shredded
2 tablespoons water
3 tablespoons butter
1 tablespoon sugar
1 tablespoon lemon juice
Salt and pepper
Chopped parsley
Caraway seeds (sparingly)

Melt butter in deep skillet or saucepan; add water, celery and cabbage and cover with heavy lid. Steam for about 10 minutes until tender (lifting contents from bottom of pan with spatula occasionally to steam evenly). Add lemon juice, salt, pepper and sugar and continue steaming very slowly until tender. Add yogurt and heat through, or top with yogurt mixed with caraway seeds.

Note: Summer squash may be prepared the same way.

Hot vegetables served with cold yogurt are a taste and temperature sensation—unique and exotic.

Zucchini w/yogurt & cheese

Yogurt
1 pound zucchini (small)
6 eggs
Parmesan cheese, grated fine
3 tablespoons butter or hot oil
¾ teaspoon salt
¾ teaspoon pepper

Cut zucchini into thin slices. Sauté slowly for about 10 minutes in a very large skillet until tender (not too soft). Beat eggs, mix with cheese and seasonings. Pour over zucchini until eggs are cooked. Spoon enough yogurt to cover mixture and run briefly under broiler for a few minutes until light brown.

INTERNATIONAL DISHES

Iran

Here is a recipe that is popular in Iran:

>   Yogurt 3 cups
> 1½ cucumbers, peeled and grated
> ½ cup raisins, washed
> 1 cup water
>   Chives, parsley and/or dill
>   Salt and pepper

Beat yogurt and cucumber until smooth. Blend in water until mixture is the consistency of cream soup. Season to taste with salt and pepper. Stir in raisins, chives and other herbs. Chill, and just before serving, garnish with egg slices. This makes a delicious soup, or can be served as a drink for an opening course.

Note: The above recipe is very easy to prepare in an electric blender.

India

Here is a concoction considered a delicacy in India:

Boil 2 large potatoes in their jackets; when cool, peel and cube. Make a dressing of 2 cups of yogurt, season with salt, 1½ teaspoons caraway seeds, and 1 teaspoon curry powder (optional). Gently stir in with the potato cubes. Let chill for a few hours before serving. Garnish with chopped chives or green onions.

Bulgaria

In Bulgaria a dish called "Moussaka" is popular:

Sprinkle 1 teaspoon salt over slices of 2 large eggplants, ¼ inch thick. In a large skillet, fry 2 finely chopped onions, 1 green pepper, chopped, 3 minced garlic cloves in oil; add 1½ pounds of ground lamb (or beef), separating into particles with a fork. Season with salt, pepper, paprika and brown well. Remove from skillet and set aside.

Dip eggplant slices in flour and brown on both sides in same pan. In a casserole arrange alternate layers of eggplant slices and meat mixture; bake at 350° F. for about 1 hour.

In a bowl, mix 2 cups yogurt, 3 egg yolks and ½ cup sifted flour; spoon over contents of the casserole; pass it briefly under the flames of the broiler for a custard-like topping.

FRUITS & DESSERTS

Dessert elegant

Below is a delicious and unique dessert we found in a very plush restaurant on the West Coast and a very plush price indeed. The service, which included attractive glass dishes, added to the festivities. You can do the same thing at home inexpensively, and it will be fun to eat, too.

    Strawberries
    Raw sugar
    Yogurt

Wash but do not hull strawberries. Chill thoroughly. Serve to each person in separate bowls strawberries, small dish for raw sugar and dish for yogurt. Dip berries in sugar and then in yogurt.

Simple rice pudding

4 cups milk
2 tablespoons rice
1 cup yogurt
Pinch of salt
1 tablespoon sugar
Cinnamon
Raisins (optional)

Bring milk to boil; boil very slowly for a few minutes; add rice, salt, and sugar and continue boiling at very low heat until milk is reduced to about half. Stir every once in a while. Pour pudding into shallow glass dish, add washed and drained raisins, mix well; sprinkle generously with cinnamon. Let stand until cool. Refrigerate for several hours. Top with yogurt sweetened with a little powdered sugar and ½ teaspoon vanilla. This is a different kind of a rice pudding.

Yogurt ice box pudding

 2 cups yogurt
   Plain cake (pound)
 2 cups sliced bananas, berries,
   peaches, etc.
½ cup sugar
½ cup maraschino cherries

Line Pyrex dish with cake. Mix fruit with sugar. Fold yogurt into fruit. Top with cherries and refrigerate for several hours before serving.

Fruit sherbet No. 1

2 cups yogurt
1 small can frozen concentrated fruit
   juice
2 teaspoons vanilla

Combine all ingredients, mix well and place in refrigerator tray to freeze.

Note: Fruits may be grape juice, orange juice or any of the concentrated fruit juices.

Fruit sherbet No. 2

1 cup yogurt
½ cup orange juice
¼ cup corn syrup
1 tablespoon lemon juice
2 egg whites

Combine ingredients. Freeze in refrigerator tray until particles of ice begin to form around tray. Remove to bowl and beat until smooth. Beat egg whites until stiff. Fold into mixture. Return to tray to freeze.

Healthful dessert

Bananas, oranges
Nuts

Whip ½ cup of yogurt with ½ cup mayonnaise into a creamy consistency and spoon generously over fruit and nuts.

The *American Journal of Digestive Diseases* in an article entitled "Effect of Yogurt with Prune Whip on Constipation" has stated that yogurt combined with prune whip is a great aid in alleviating constipation. Prunes that have been soaked in cold water, pitted and combined with yogurt and thoroughly mixed in an electric blender provide an excellent method of using health-giving foods to do away with constipation.

Prune whip w/yogurt

1 cup prune pulp
2 egg whites
2 tablespoons lemon juice
1 cup sugar
1 cup yogurt

Wash prunes, cover with cold water and cook until soft. Drain, remove stones and mash fine or put through grinder. Measure 1 cup of the pulp, add half of the sugar, lemon juice, and cook for a few minutes or until thick. When cool, beat egg whites, adding remaining sugar gradually until stiff but not dry. Fold egg whites into prune whip. Spoon whip into individual dishes and chill. Top with yogurt—the contrasting flavors add piquancy.

Note: Apricot whip is prepared the same way.

Jell-o yogurt dessert

1 package flavored gelatin
1 cup hot water
1 scant cup cold water (or ice cubes
  for speedy cooling)
1 level teaspoon plain gelatin
¾ cup yogurt
1 cup fruit cocktail, drained
  Maraschino cherries

Combine flavored gelatin and hot water. Float plain gelatin on cold water to soften—combine; when cold, add yogurt and beat in blender for 2 seconds; add fruit cocktail. In a mold, place maraschino cherries and add gelatin mixture. Refrigerate for several hours until firm.

Note: Lime or orange-banana Jello are good flavors for this recipe and are a delight to the eye.

CAKES MUFFINS PIES, BISCUITS

Quick coffee cake

    1 cup sugar
    2 cups flour
    1 teaspoon soda
    2 teaspoons baking powder
 ¼ cup butter (or margarine)
    1 egg, beaten
    1 scant cup of yogurt

TOPPING
    Sugar, 3 teaspoons
    Cinnamon, 3 teaspoons

Mix and sift dry ingredients. Cut in butter with pastry blender or two knives. Add egg and yogurt. Beat thoroughly. Pour half the batter into a greased pan, sprinkle half the sugar mixture over batter. Add remainder of batter and sprinkle with sugar mixture. Bake in moderately hot oven (375° F.) about 40 minutes.

Upside-down cake

Prepare above batter. Spread 3 tablespoons melted butter in cake pan; add ¼ cup brown sugar; sprinkle with a little cinnamon. Arrange sliced, canned pineapple over butter mixture. Pour cake batter over fruit and bake as above.

Variation: Apples sliced, or peaches halved, may be substituted.

Try making biscuits with yogurt instead of sweet milk:

Biscuits

    2 cups flour
    2 teaspoons baking powder
  ½ teaspoon soda
    1 teaspoon salt
    4 tablespoons shortening
  ¾ cup yogurt (about)

Sift dry ingredients twice. Cut in shortening with pastry blender until mixture resembles coarse corn meal. Stir in with fork enough yogurt to make soft dough; keep stirring until all the flour disappears.

Turn out dough on floured board; pat dough or roll out ½ inch thick; dip biscuit cutter in flour and cut. Bake on greased baking sheet in hot oven (450° F.) 12 to 15 minutes.

Corn muffins

1 cup corn meal
1 cup flour.
3 teaspoons baking powder
½ teaspoon soda
½ teaspoon salt
3 tablespoons sugar
¼ cup butter
2 egg yolks
2 egg whites
1 cup yogurt

Sift dry ingredients together to blend thoroughly. Cut in butter with pastry blender (until mixture resembles the size of small peas). Add egg yolks and yogurt.

Mix just enough to hold mixture together. Fold in egg whites beaten stiff but not dry. Place in well-greased muffin tins ⅔ full. Bake 20 to 30 minutes (depending on size) in hot oven (400° F.).

Raisin muffins

   ¼ cup shortening
    3 tablespoons sugar
    2 tablespoons molasses
    1 egg, unbeaten
1½ cups sifted flour
   ½ teaspoon double-acting baking
      powder
    1 teaspoon soda
   ½ teaspoon salt
   ¾ cup buckwheat groats (packaged)
    1 cup yogurt
   ¼ cup seeded raisins

Cream shortening, sugar and molasses until light and fluffy. Beat in egg. Sift flour, baking powder, soda and salt; blend into shortening mixture. Add groats, yogurt and raisins; mix until dry ingredients are moistened. Bake in hot oven (425°F.) 20 minutes, or until browned.

Convenience package mix

     1 package gingerbread mix
     ¾ cup yogurt
     ¼ cup water

Place mix in large bowl. In another bowl, beat yogurt with water. Follow mixing and baking directions from package.

Fast, tangy apple upside-down cake

5 apples, peeled and sliced
4 tablespoons butter
1 cup brown sugar
1 teaspoon cinnamon
½ cup yogurt
1 package yellow cake mix (net wt. 9 ounces)
1 egg
¼ teaspoon baking soda
1 teaspoon vanilla

Melt shortening in 8-inch glass baking dish, blend thoroughly with sugar; cover with sliced apples, sprinkle with cinnamon. Set aside.

Place cake mix in bowl. In a smaller bowl beat egg with yogurt well. Add half of liquid mixture to mix. Beat according to directions on package. Add remaining half of liquid mixture, soda, and vanilla. Bake according to directions on package.

Note: Pineapple upside-down cake may be made with the same method, substituting canned sliced pineapple.

119

Yogurt cake

Sift together 1 cup flour, 1 teaspoon baking powder. Beat 4 eggs, add 1 cup sugar, beat until smooth. Stir in 1 cup yogurt, 1 teaspoon grated lemon rind, the sifted flour and baking powder. Stir until smooth. Pour into a greased 8-inch square baking pan and bake 35 minutes at 375° F.

Syrup: Prepare syrup by boiling 1½ cups sugar and 2½ cups water. Boil until thick, but not heavy (about ½ hour); add a few drops of lemon juice. Cool cake and add hot syrup, or cool syrup and pour over hot cake.

Yogurt pie

Should you ever come to California go to Hollywood, and when you get to Hollywood, pay a visit to the Farmer's Market, and when you reach the Farmer's Market order their superb delicacy—Yogurt Pie. It is truly a taste treat. It is the pride of the chef and has been and remains the most popular pie in Hollywood.

Here is how you make it:

    1 cup yogurt
    ½ pound cottage cheese (small curd,
        not creamed, sometimes called
        country style)
    1 tablespoon honey
    1 teaspoon vanilla

Bake an 8-inch pie shell. Line bottom of pie with fresh strawberries, raspberries, blackberries or sliced bananas; sprinkle with a small amount of sugar. Whip together all the ingredients listed above and fill the pie with the yogurt mixture. Serve with whipped cream if desired.

Note: This pie should be refrigerated for several hours before serving. May be prepared without the fruit filling.

ADDITIONAL RECIPES

ADDITIONAL RECIPES

ADDITIONAL RECIPES

ADDITIONAL RECIPES

ADDITIONAL RECIPES